André Butzer

Galeria Mário Sequeira, Braga
1 de Abril – 28 de Maio, 2017

Harpune Verlag, Wien

NASAHEIM in Portugal

For one of his favorite places, Braga, André Butzer together with Mário Sequeira has compiled a very fine and unique selection of works from the years 2004 to 2016. Although this selection has no right to claim any sort of completeness concerning the totality of Butzer´s art, it happens that an entire artistic inner coherence is now ready for the audience to check out, maybe in a way it was never seen before. What is NASAHEIM? It´s an utopian place of no measurable size, as this place is of no physical quality, but it is rather an irrational frequency of light that is only a threshold, a beam-like and eternal contemplation that endlessly pulsates and vibrates through space and time. Life and death is one and Butzer had his paintings travelling quite near to that frequency over the past twenty years. His duty now is to stay up there, close to the light, where darkness itself becomes mild light all in one, where finally death equals life and the golden bell is striking peacefully through night and day who are themselves complete and „one" as a whole and who are therefore permanent in durance and event. Butzer has managed to destroy all pictorial means necessary, basically he has managed to destroy the line as a constitutional, but to eventually overcome element in painting. Instead, he has come to see the beautiful fugue appearing through the law of light. This fugue is a profound negativity who gives constant birth to what a painted image is built upon: a holy plane expanding in favor of an endowment. This endowment is what connects Butzer´s art to the unison of the history of color. Color is considered a deeply fateful matter, a commemoration of centuries kept alive.

Steffen Krüger, Rangsdorf/Germany

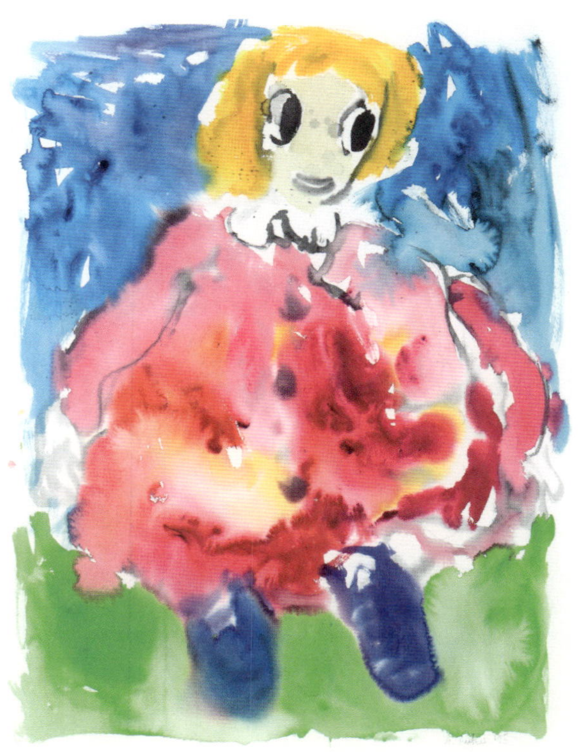

Sem titulo (Lisa), 2005
Aquarela sobre papel
76 x 56,5 cm

Sem titulo, 2014
Óleo sobre tela
46 x 34 cm

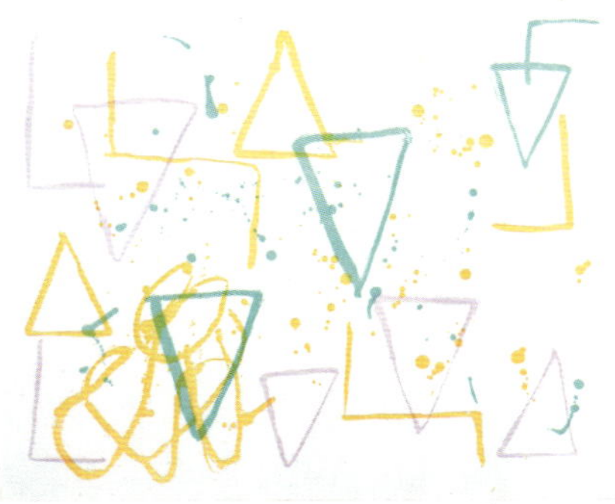

Sem titulo, 2009 - 2010
Gravura
49 x 60 cm

Sem titulo, 2004
Lápis sobre papel
17 x 24 cm

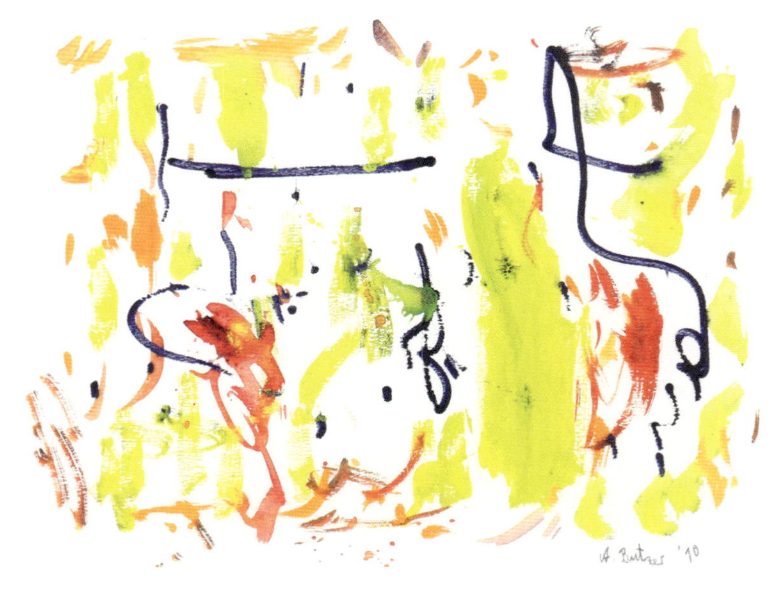

Sem titulo, 2010
Aquarela sobre papel
40 x 50 cm

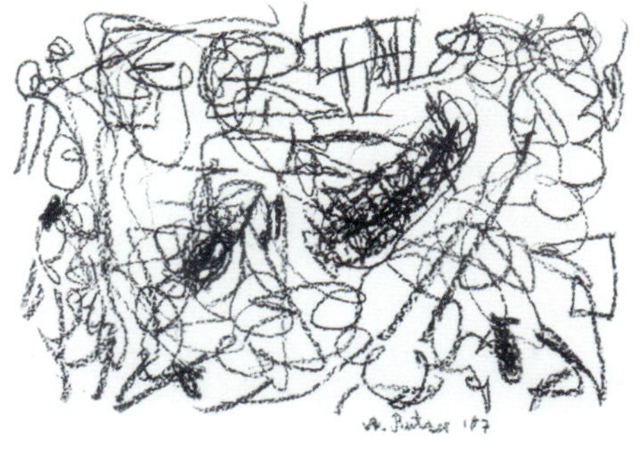

Sem titulo, 2007
Giz sobre papel
30 x 42 cm

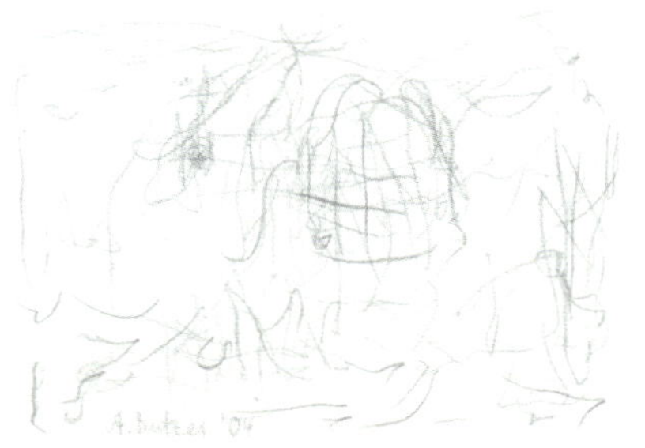

Sem titulo, 2004
Lápis sobre papel
17 x 24 cm

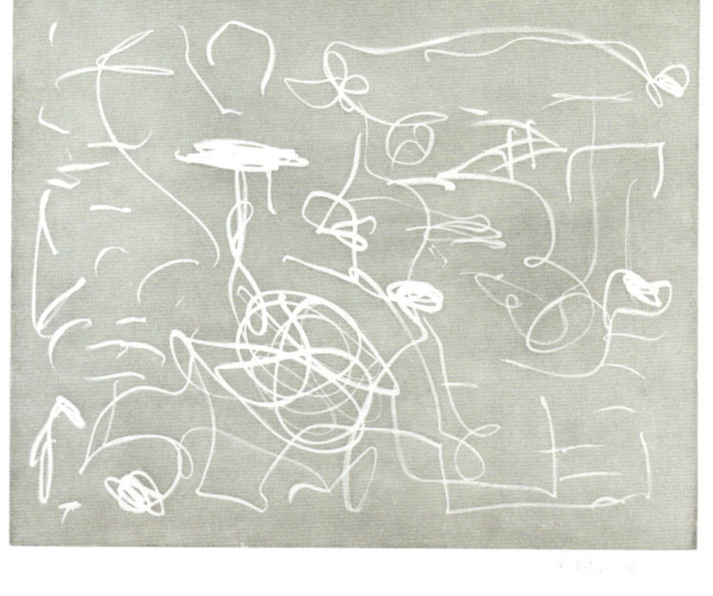

Sem titulo, 2010
Gravura
49 x 60 cm

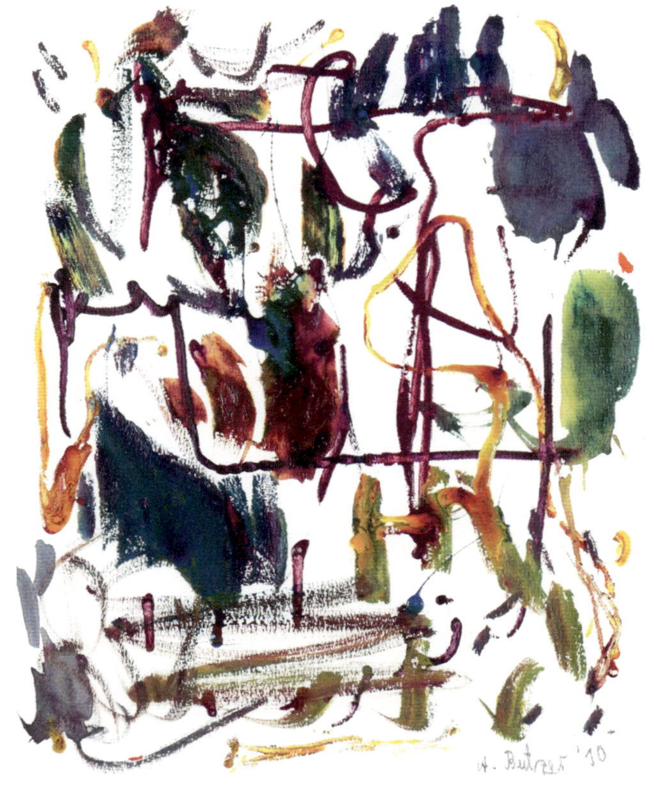

Sem titulo, 2010
Aquarela sobre papel
50 x 40 cm

Sem titulo, 2016
Óleo sobre tela
160 x 100 cm

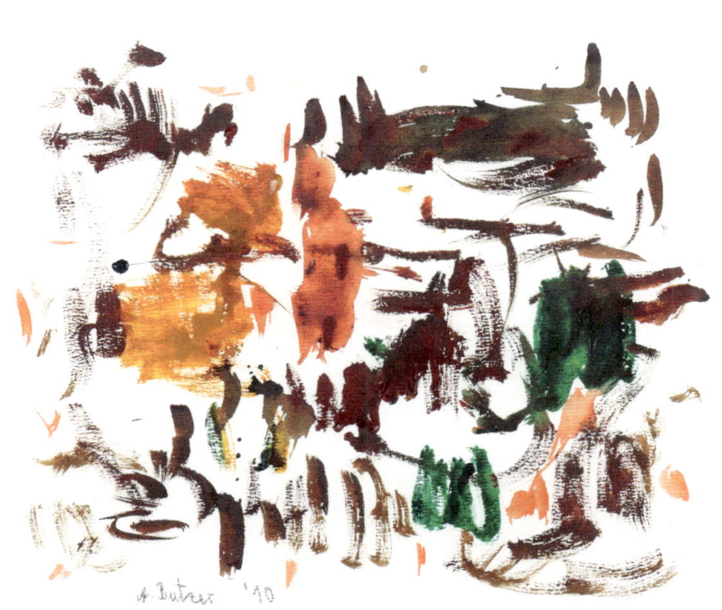

Sem titulo, 2010
Aquarela sobre papel
40 x 50 cm

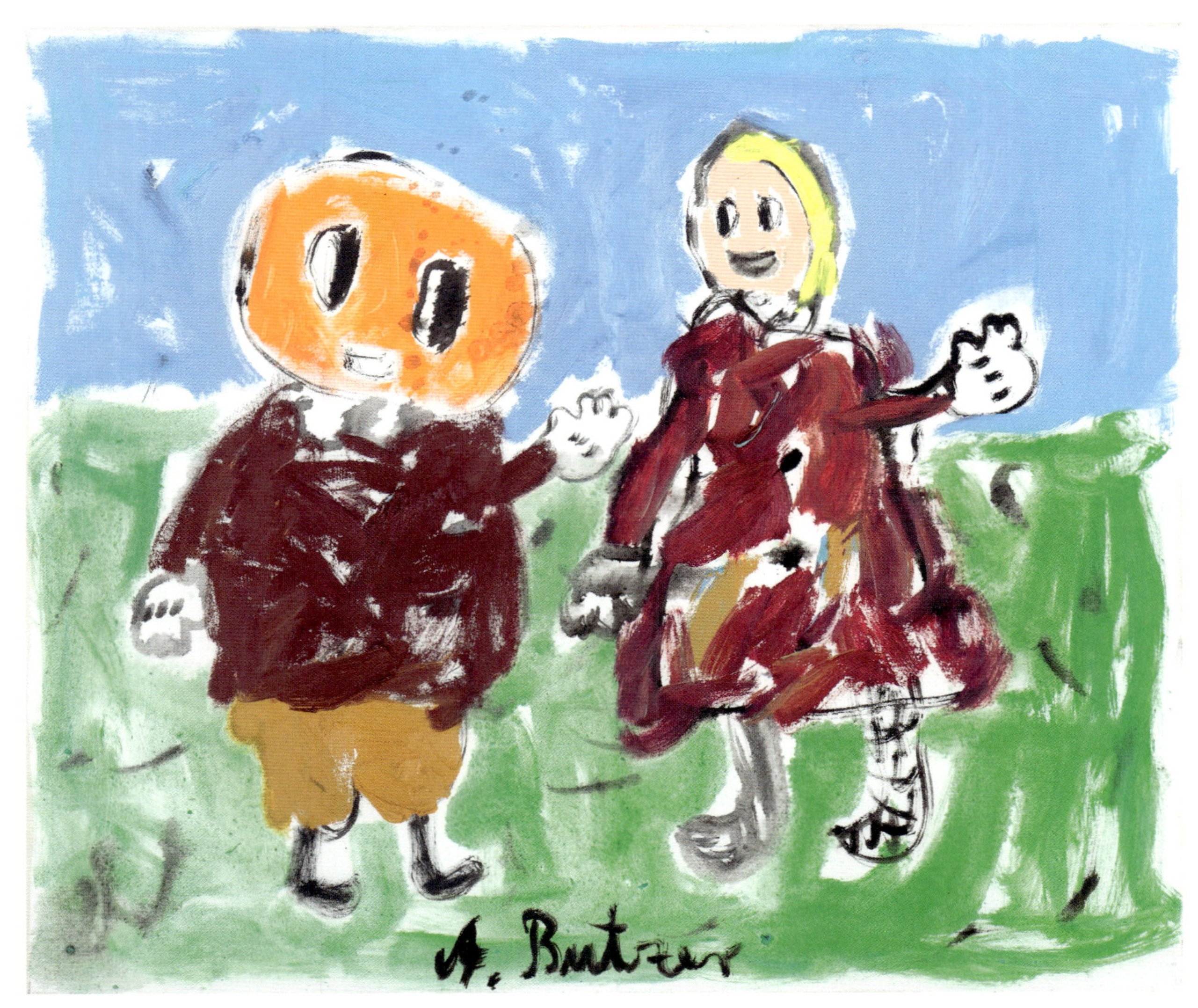

Sem titulo, 2008
Óleo sobre tela
60 x 70 cm

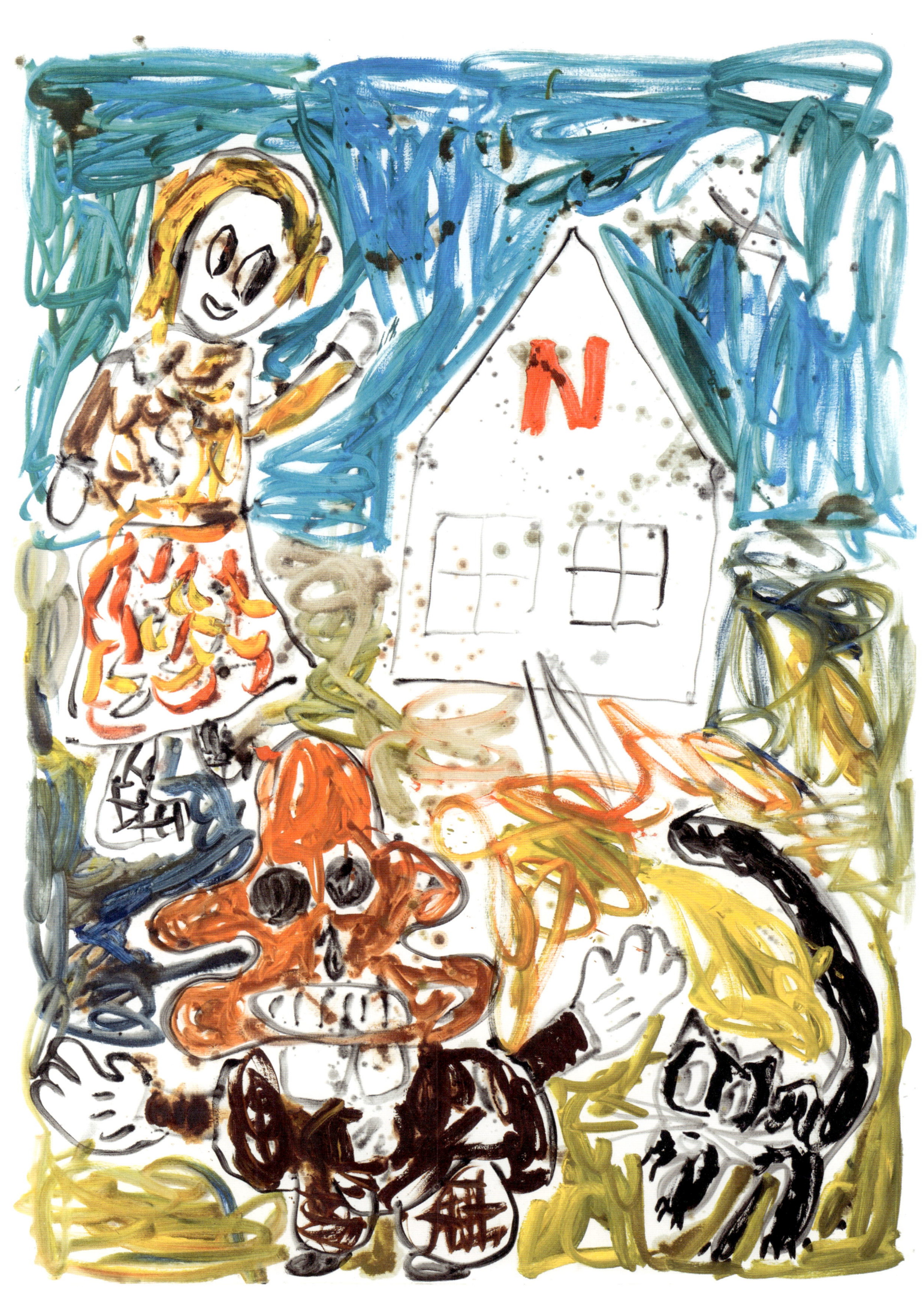

Sem titulo, 2007
Óleo sobre tela
200 x 140 cm

Sem titulo, 2012
Têmpera sobre tela
80 x 100 cm

Sem titulo, 2013
Óleo sobre tela
80 x 80 cm

Galeria Mário Sequeira

Quinta da Igreja
Rua da Galeria 129
4700-803 Parada de Tibães
Braga – Portugal
T + 351-253-602-550
www.mariosequeira.com

André Butzer

1 de Abril – 28 de Maio, 2017

Fotografias: Marco Mendes, Braga
Impressão: Druckerei Kettler, Alemanha
700 exemplares

ISBN 978-3-903348-09-7

Harpune Verlag KG, Vienna, 2017